KID CHEMISTRY LAB

INSPECTING ELEMENTS & THE PERIODIC TABLE

Jessica Rusick

Checkerboard Library
An Imprint of Abdo Publishing
abdobooks.com

ABDOBOOKS.COM
Published by Abdo Publishing, a division of ABDO, PO Box 398166, Minneapolis, Minnesota 55439.

Printed in the United States of America, North Mankato, Minnesota
052022
092022

THIS BOOK CONTAINS RECYCLED MATERIALS

Design and Production: Kelly Doudna, Mighty Media, Inc.
Editor: Liz Salzmann
Cover Photograph: max-kegfire/iStockphoto
Interior Photographs: Bjoern Wylezich/Shutterstock Images, p. 25; CRStocker/Shutterstock Images, p. 5; Designua/Shutterstock Images, p. 13; Diego Grandi/Shutterstock Images, p. 23; Heritage Image Partnership Ltd/Alamy Photo, p. 9; julie deshaies/Shutterstock Images, pp. 16–17; Mighty Media, Inc., pp. 26, 27, 28, 29; MR.ANUWAT/Shutterstock Images, p. 15; Prostock-studio/Shutterstock Images, p. 7; Sergey Novikov/Shutterstock Images, p. 11; Volgi archive/Alamy Photo, p. 19; Wikimedia Commons, p. 21

Library of Congress Control Number: 2021953158

Publisher's Cataloging-in-Publication Data
Names: Rusick, Jessica, author.
Title: Inspecting elements & the periodic table / by Jessica Rusick.
Description: Minneapolis, Minnesota : Abdo Publishing, 2023 | Series: Kid chemistry lab | Includes online resources and index.
Identifiers: ISBN 9781532199011 (lib. bdg.) | ISBN 9781098272944 (ebook)
Subjects: LCSH: Chemistry--Juvenile literature. | Chemical elements--Juvenile literature. | Periodic table of the elements--Juvenile literature. | Science projects--Juvenile literature.
Classification: DDC 540--dc23

CONTENTS

Chapter 1

WHAT ARE ELEMENTS?

An element is a substance that can't be broken down into simpler substances. Elements make up all matter. Gold, helium, oxygen, and iron are all elements. Our bodies are mostly made of four elements. These are oxygen, nitrogen, hydrogen, and carbon.

Chemistry is the study of matter and elements. Scientists called chemists study what matter is made of, how it behaves, and how it interacts with other matter. There are 118 known elements. Every element is listed on the periodic table of the elements. The periodic table organizes elements based on their **properties**.

STATES OF MATTER

Elements can be liquids, solids, or gases. These are the main states of matter. Changes in temperature can cause elements to change states.

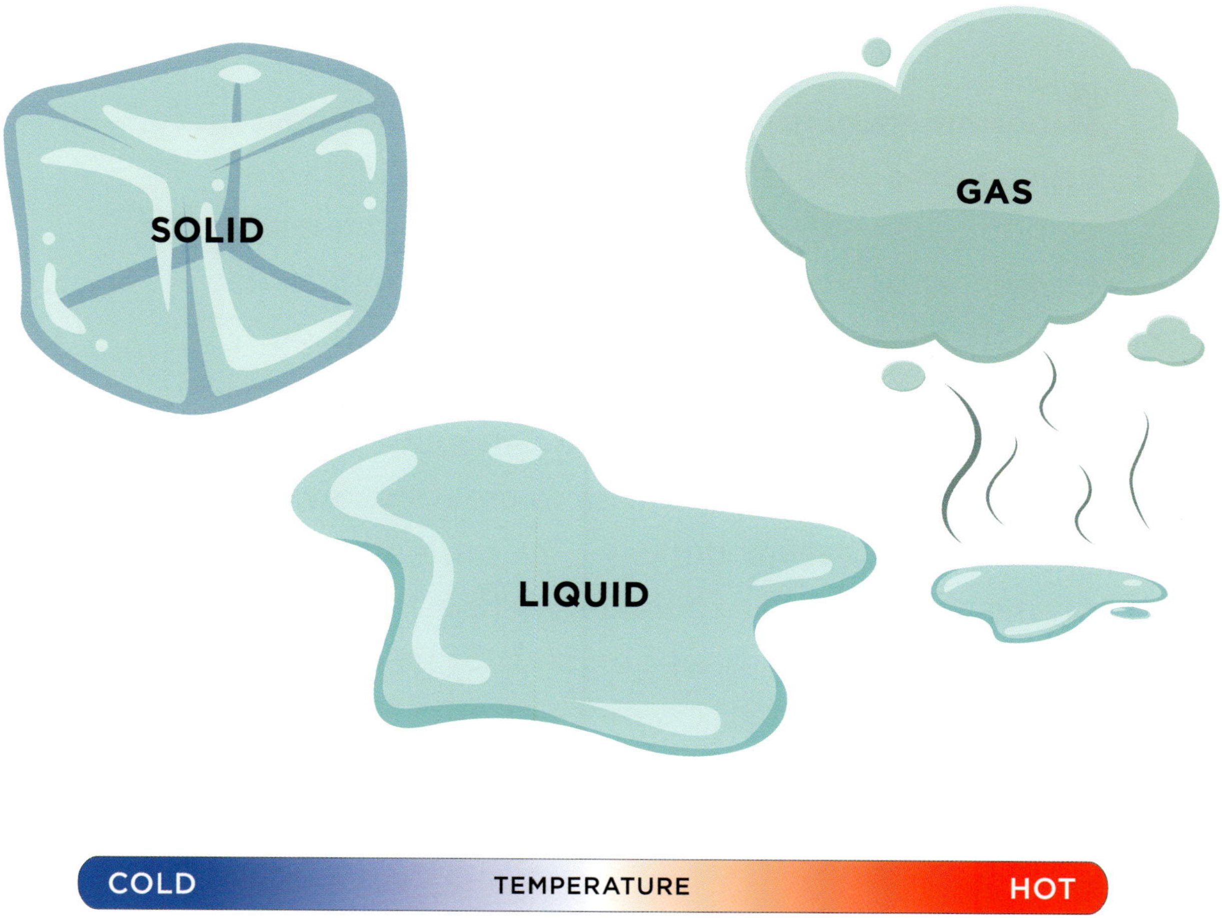

Chapter 2

ELEMENTS BASICS

Different elements can bond to form new substances called compounds. There are millions of different compounds. Sugar is one example. It is made of carbon, oxygen, and hydrogen. Compounds have different **properties** than the elements they are made of.

Chemists study elements and compounds to learn about the human body and the natural world. Studying elements also allows chemists to create stronger tools, building materials, and more. The periodic table helps chemists study and experiment with elements. Chemists can quickly find information about an element using the table. It can also help chemists **predict** which elements will form compounds.

The salt used in cooking is a compound. It is made of the elements sodium and chlorine.

Chapter 3

HISTORY OF ELEMENTS

Humans have studied elements for thousands of years. Some ancient Greek philosophers believed everything was made of water, earth, fire, and air. They called these elements.

In the 1660s, Irish chemist Robert Boyle developed the modern **definition** of an element. In the 1770s, French chemist Antoine-Laurent Lavoisier made a list of elements based on Boyle's definition. Since then, scientists have identified more elements. They also worked to organize elements by their **characteristics**.

In 1869, Russian scientist Dmitri Mendeleev developed the basis for the modern periodic table. It had 56 elements organized into rows and columns. Scientists have since added to and rearranged Mendeleev's table as they discovered new elements.

Mendeleev's table helped scientists understand how elements behave. Mendeleev even used his table to predict properties of undiscovered elements!

Chapter 4

INSIDE AN ELEMENT

Elements are made of tiny pieces of matter called atoms. Atoms are made of even smaller bits. These are protons, electrons, and neutrons. All atoms of an element have the same number of protons. This is the element's atomic number. All helium atoms, for example, have two protons. So, 2 is helium's atomic number.

Atoms have the same number of electrons as protons. So, an element's atomic number also indicates how many electrons its atoms have. Electrons move around the inside of an atom in layers called shells. The first, innermost shell holds up to two electrons. Outer shells can hold eight electrons each.

Helium is one of the lightest elements. One of its main uses is to fill balloons so they float in the air.

When an atom's outermost shell is full, it is considered stable. Atoms bond with each other to become stable. When bonding, atoms give, receive, or share electrons until they are stable.

When elements bond with each other, they form molecules called compounds. For example, water is a compound. A water molecule is made of two hydrogen atoms and one oxygen atom. The elements share electrons to form the compound.

WATER MOLECULE FORMATION

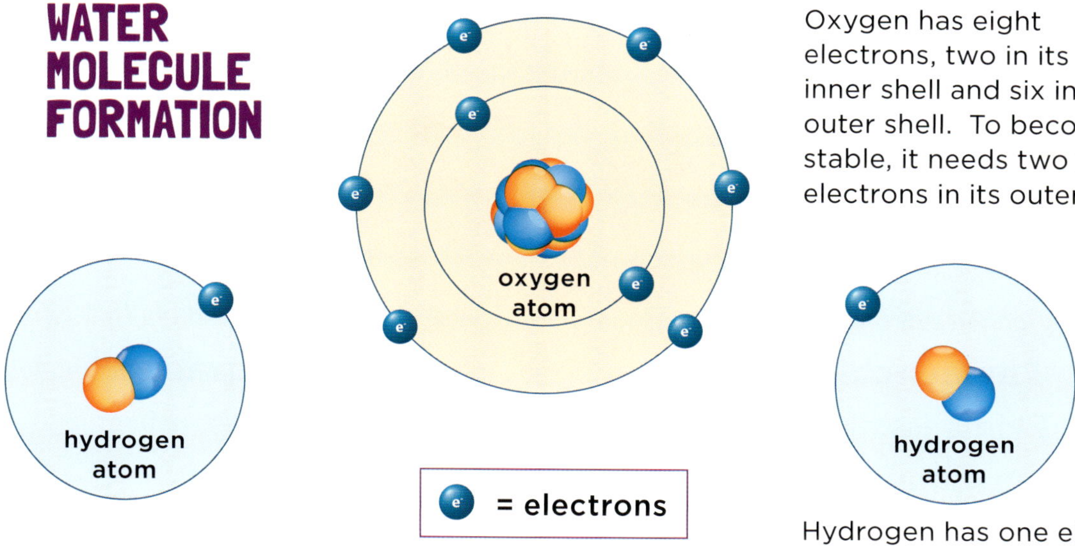

Oxygen has eight electrons, two in its inner shell and six in the outer shell. To become stable, it needs two more electrons in its outer shell.

Hydrogen has one electron in its only shell. It needs one more to be stable.

In a water molecule, one oxygen atom bonds with two hydrogen atoms. The atoms share electrons to become stable.

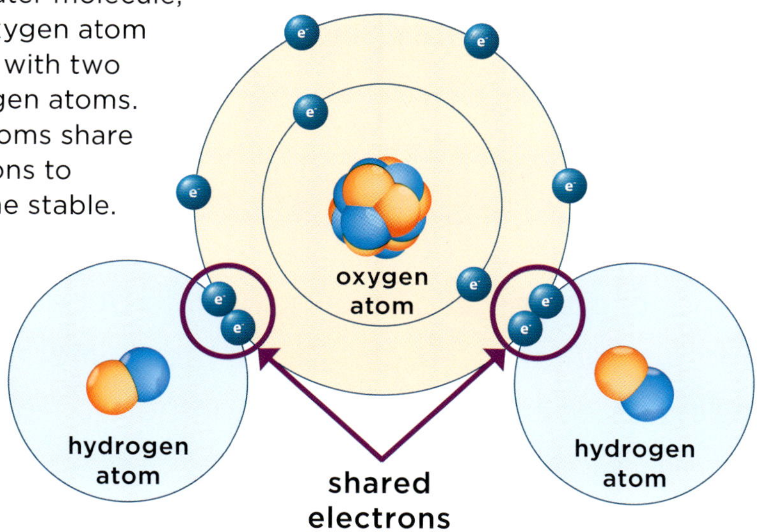

Chapter 5

TYPES OF ELEMENTS

The periodic table has several levels of organization. Elements are divided into three main **categories**. Most are metals. They are found on the left side of the table. Metals are usually shiny and hard. They conduct electricity well and only melt at high temperatures. Copper, gold, iron, and titanium are all metal elements.

Other elements are nonmetals. They are found mostly on the right side of the table. Nonmetals are not shiny and do not conduct electricity well. Many nonmetals are gases. These include oxygen, helium, and neon. Carbon and sulfur are examples of solid nonmetals. Most solid nonmetals are **brittle**.

Six elements are metalloids. They fall in between metals and nonmetals on the periodic table. Metalloids have **properties** of both metals and nonmetals. Silicon

Silicon is used to make microchips for electronics such as computers and cell phones.

is a metalloid. It is shiny and **brittle**. It can also conduct electricity.

Each element on the periodic table is represented by one or two letters. This is the element's chemical symbol. Often, the chemical symbol is the first letter or letters of the element's name. Oxygen is *O*. Calcium is *Ca*. Some elements' symbols come from Latin. For example, gold's symbol is *Au* because gold's Latin name is *aurum*.

PERIODIC TABLE

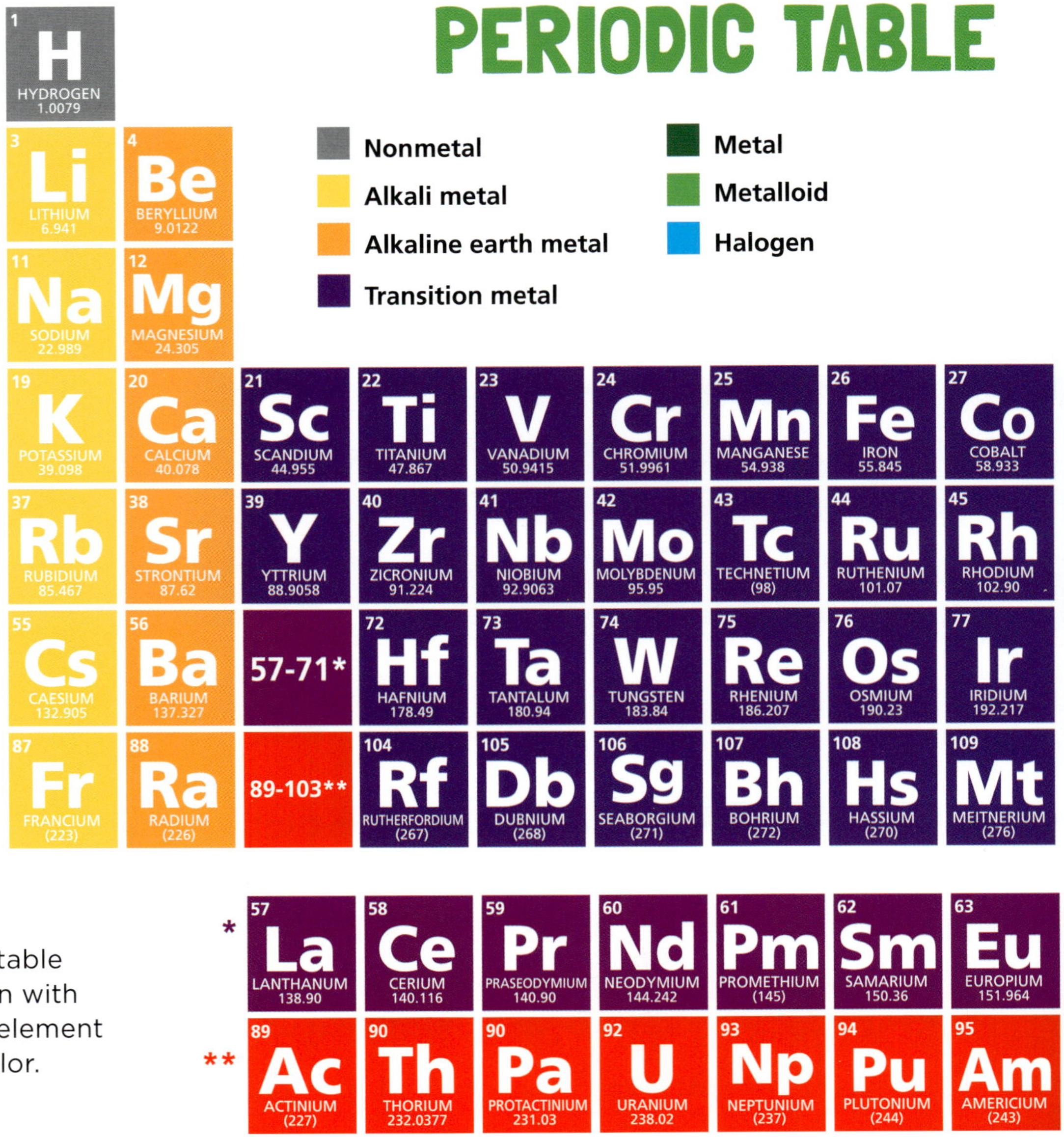

The periodic table is often shown with each type of element a different color.

OF THE ELEMENTS

- Noble gas
- Actinide
- Lanthanide

								2 He HELIUM 4.0026
			5 B BORON 10.811	6 C CARBON 12.011	7 N NITROGEN 14.007	8 O OXYGEN 15.999	9 F FLUORINE 18.998	10 Ne NEON 20.1797
			13 Al ALUMINIUM 26.981	14 Si SILICON 28.085	15 P PHOSPHORUS 30.974	16 S SULFUR 32.066	17 Cl CHLORINE 35.453	18 Ar ARGON 39.948
28 Ni NICKEL 58.6934	29 Cu COPPER 63.546	30 Zn ZINC 65.38	31 Ga GALLIUM 69.723	32 Ge GERMANIUM 72.63	33 As ARSENIC 74.921	34 Se SELENIUM 78.971	35 Br BROMINE 79.904	36 Kr KRYPTON 83.798
46 Pd PALLADIUM 106.42	47 Ag SILVER 107.8682	48 Cd CADMIUM 112.414	49 In INDIUM 114.818	50 Sn TIN 118.710	51 Sb ANTIMONY 121.760	52 Te TELLURIUM 127.60	53 I IODINE 126.90	54 Xe XENON 131.293
78 Pt PLATINUM 195.084	79 Au GOLD 196.96	80 Hg MERCURY 200.59	81 Tl THALLIUM 204.38	82 Pb LEAD 207.2	83 Bi BISMUTH 208.98	84 Po POLONIUM (209)	85 At ASTATINE (210)	86 Rn RADON (222)
110 Ds DARMSTADTIUM (281)	111 Rg ROENTGENIUM (280)	112 Cn COPERNICIUM (285)	113 Uut UNUNTRIUM (284)	114 Fl FLEROVIUM (289)	115 Uup UNUNPENTIUM (288)	116 Lv LIVERMORIUM (293)	117 Ts TENNESSINE (294)	118 Og OGANESSON (294)

64 Gd GADOLINIUM 157.25	65 Tb TERIBIUM 158.92	66 Dy DYSPROSIUM 162.500	67 Ho HOLMIUM 164.93	68 Er ERBIUM 167.259	69 Tm THULIUM 168.93	70 Yb YTTERBIUM 173.054	71 Lu LUTETIUM 174.9668
96 Cm CURIUM (247)	97 Bk BERKELIUM (247)	98 Cf CALIFORNIUM (251)	99 Es EINSTEINIUM (252)	100 Fm FERMIUM (257)	101 Md MENDELEVIUM (258)	102 No NOBELIUM (259)	103 Lr LAWRENCIUM (262)

Chapter 6

PERIODS & GROUPS

Elements on the periodic table are organized from left to right by atomic number. The periodic table is also divided into rows and columns. The rows are called periods. An element's period number tells you how many electron shells it has. Oxygen is in the second period. So, its atoms have two electron shells.

There are 18 columns, called groups. Elements in each group have similar **properties**. The elements in group 18, for example, are called noble gases. These include helium and neon. Noble gases all have full outer electron shells. This means they do not naturally bond with other elements.

In 1898, German chemist Hugo Erdmann became the first to use the term *noble gas*.

Chapter 7

NATURAL ELEMENTS

Most elements are found naturally on Earth. Earth's crust contains mostly oxygen, silicon, and aluminum. It also has small amounts of many other elements.

Some elements exist in a pure form. For example, pieces of pure gold can be found in rock. But most elements don't exist in a pure form. They must be chemically separated from other substances. Aluminum comes from bauxite rocks. Bauxite is first **refined** into a compound containing aluminum and oxygen. Then the oxygen is removed, leaving only aluminum.

Scientists have discovered new elements by studying natural substances. Polish chemist Marie Curie and her husband, Pierre, discovered the element radium in the early 1900s. Curie **isolated** radium from a type of rock called pitchblende.

Marie Curie was the first woman to win a Nobel Prize. She was also the first person to win the award twice.

Chapter 8

SYNTHETIC ELEMENTS

Some elements on the periodic table are synthetic. Synthetic elements do not occur naturally on Earth. They are made by scientists in laboratories.

Scientists use particle accelerators to create new elements. This type of machine smashes atoms together at high speeds. The **collisions** force the atoms to combine into new elements. One synthetic element is mendelevium. It was created in 1955 by a team of scientists in Berkeley, California. The element is named after Dmitri Mendeleev.

Most synthetic elements can only be made in small amounts. So, they do not have many practical uses. Scientists mostly use synthetic elements for research.

The largest particle accelerator is the Large Hadron Collider. It is located on the border between France and Switzerland, under the main laboratory of the European Organization for Nuclear Research.

Chapter 9

ISOTOPES & ALLOTROPES

Elements have several different forms. These are called isotopes. An element's isotopes have the same number of protons, but different numbers of neutrons. Carbon has three isotopes. The most common form has six neutrons. Another has seven neutrons. The third has eight neutrons.

An element's isotopes each have different **properties**. For example, a carbon atom that has six or seven neutrons is stable. This means it does not decay, or break down. Carbon atoms with eight neutrons are unstable. They decay into other elements over time.

Sometimes, an element's atoms bond together in different ways. This creates different forms of an element

Diamond is the hardest natural substance. It forms hundreds of miles underground. The extreme heat and pressure there turn carbon into diamond. This process can take more than 1 billion years.

called allotropes. Carbon has several allotropes. One is diamond. Another is graphite, which is used to make pencil lead. The substances look very different. But they are both made of pure carbon!

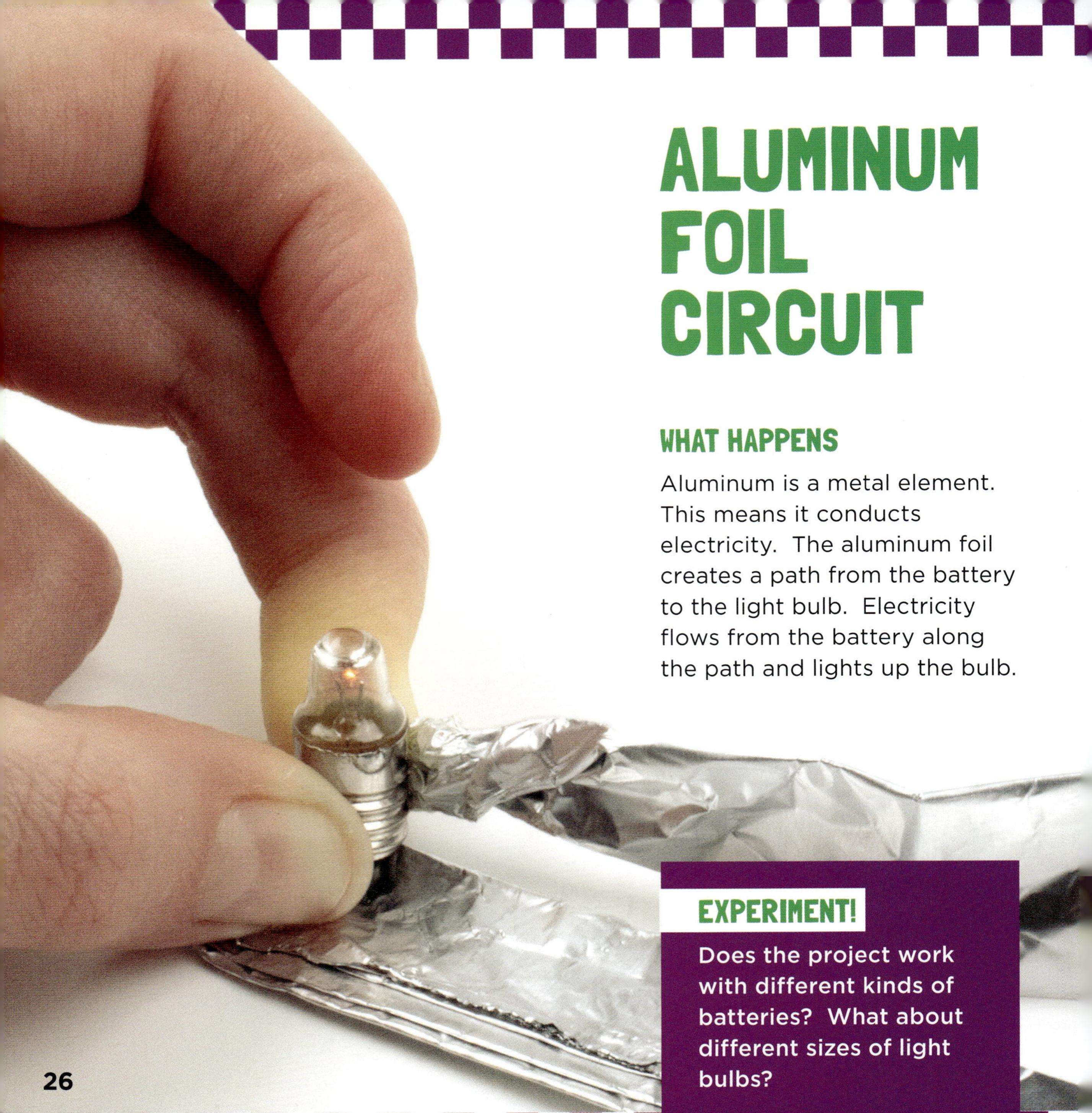

ALUMINUM FOIL CIRCUIT

WHAT HAPPENS

Aluminum is a metal element. This means it conducts electricity. The aluminum foil creates a path from the battery to the light bulb. Electricity flows from the battery along the path and lights up the bulb.

EXPERIMENT!

Does the project work with different kinds of batteries? What about different sizes of light bulbs?

MATERIALS

- aluminum foil
- ruler
- tape
- D battery
- small light bulb

STEPS

1 Tear off two 6-inch (15 cm) pieces of aluminum foil.

2 Fold each piece **lengthwise** into strips that are about ½ inch (1.25 cm) wide.

3 Tape one end of a strip to one end of the battery. Tape one end of the other strip to the other end of the battery.

4 Touch the loose end of one strip to the metal tip of the light bulb.

5 Touch the loose end of the other strip to the metal part of the bulb, close to the glass. Watch the bulb light up!

1

2

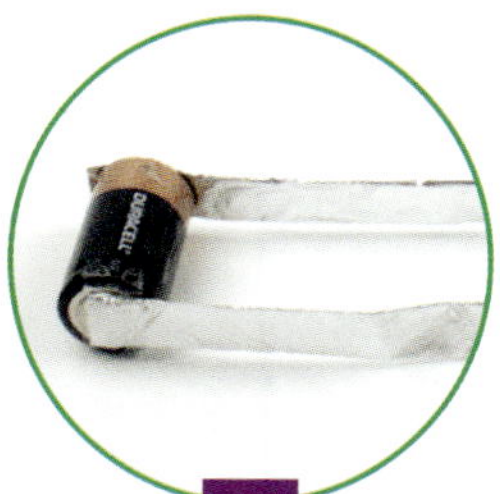

3

THE SCIENTIFIC METHOD

Want to experiment like a real chemist? Follow the scientific method! The scientific method is a process scientists use to answer questions.

1. Ask a question. Research your question to learn more about it.
2. Develop a **hypothesis**. This is your best guess about the answer to your question.
3. Experiment to test your hypothesis. Record what happens during the experiment.
4. Review the results of your experiment to draw a conclusion. Was your hypothesis supported? Why or why not? Share your results with others.

METAL FOR BREAKFAST

WHAT HAPPENS

Iron is an important part of our diet. It helps blood carry oxygen through our bodies. Many breakfast cereals include added iron that is safe to eat. Breaking down cereal in water **extracts** the iron. Since iron is magnetic, it is attracted to the magnet through the bottom of the container!

MATERIALS

- strong magnet
- tape
- clear plastic container with lid
- cereal with a high iron content
- measuring cup
- plastic bag
- water
- bowl

STEPS

1 Tape the magnet to the bottom of the container.

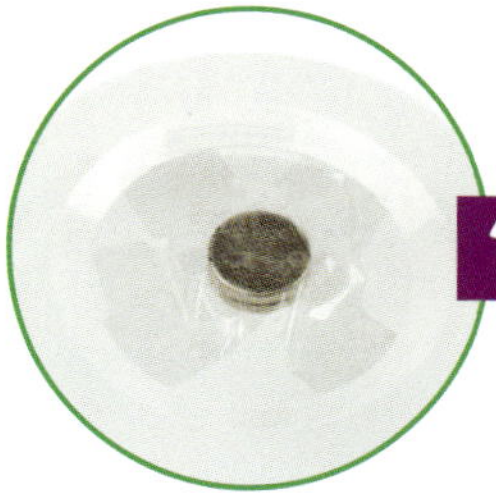

1

2 Put about 1 cup of cereal in a plastic bag. Crush the cereal into small pieces.

2

3 Pour the crushed cereal into the container. Add water to create a soupy cereal mixture.

3

4 Put the lid on the container. Shake the container for several minutes.

5 Pour the cereal mixture into a bowl. Look at what's left in the bottom of the container where the magnet is taped.

EXPERIMENT!

Repeat the steps with other cereals. Do they contain iron? What about other foods? Do some foods appear to have more iron than others?

GLOSSARY

brittle—hard but easily broken.

category—a group of people or things that are similar in some way.

characteristic—a quality or a feature of something.

collision—when two things come together with force.

definition—the meaning of a word.

extract—to withdraw by a physical or chemical process.

hypothesis (hye-PAH-thi-sis)—an unproven idea or theory based on known facts that leads to further study.

isolate—to separate one substance from another substance.

lengthwise—in the direction of the longest side.

predict—to guess something ahead of time on the basis of observation, experience, or reasoning.

property—a special quality or feature of something.

refine—to remove unwanted substances from something.

synthetic—human-made by a chemical process. Synthetic products include plastic and many kinds of fabrics, dyes, and drugs.

ONLINE RESOURCES

Booklinks
NONFICTION NETWORK
FREE! ONLINE NONFICTION RESOURCES

To learn more about elements and the periodic table, please visit **abdobooklinks.com** or scan this QR code. These links are routinely monitored and updated to provide the most current information available.

INDEX